CAN YOU SEE YOURSELF

In My Mirror

P. Utley Bradford

TrubuPRESS is a subsidiary of the Trubu Media Group whose interests include but are not limited to fiction and non fiction stories from the black experience throughout the American and African Diaspora.

Publisher: TrubuPRESS
Editor: Neo Blaqness
Cover Design: TrubuPRESS
Cover Photo Credit: Frank J. Bradford Sr.
Proofreader: Tamika Coleman

CAN YOU SEE YOURSELF IN MY MIRROR
Copyright © 2006, 2012 P. Utley Bradford

All rights reserved. No part of this book may be reproduced or transmitted in any form or by any means without written permission from the author. Permission is granted for brief excerpts to be published for book reviews.

To order, CAN YOU SEE YOURSELF IN MY MIRROR, visit http://putleybradford.trubupress.com or call (872) 22TRUBU.

Booksellers: Retail discounts are available from TrubuPRESS. Inquires about volume orders can be made via the phone number listed above.

ISBN-13: 978-0615769127
ISBN-10: 0615769128
Published by TrubuPRESS
PRINTED IN THE UNITED STATES

Dedication

TO MY GRANDS & GREATS

TYSON, TARON, DARON, JAYSON,
COLETTE, JAZMINE, DARIN JR., LAMAR,
DOMINIQUE, AKYHLA, RYKYN,
JORDYN, KERMIT, DEANN, LAVONNI,
KEVIN, KAYLA, KIRK,
IMANI, GLORIA, JADA, XAVIER,
MAYA, MORGAN, JON JR., MADISON,
TYSON JR., JA'MIR, JAVOHN, JAH'ZELLE,
AH'MIR, KHYAIN,
KASON, LYREA VI

Always know that you are a peculiar people, a royal priesthood- A holy nation and with Christ all things are possible. Much love and peace to you all.
The curse is broken.

CONTENTS

My Ministry   p.15

A Dovely Conversation   p.17

An Heir   p.19

Under Reconstruction   p.23

The Devil Goes to Church   p.25

Stolen Treasures   p.27

Broken In All The Right Places   p.29

Love Took a Ride   p.31

The 3 I Thought I knew   p.35

Living Phat   p.37

Disappointed—Not Angry   p.39

Her Apple But Your Choice   p.41

Not So Pretty   p.43

I Nearly Talked Myself to Death   p.45

All Up In My Business– Jesus Set Me Up   p.47

The Gardener   p.51

This is My Story– Not a Pretty Song   p.53

No Longer Nasty   p.57

The Old Fashioned Way p.61
Turn The World Off p.63
Not Yours p.65
There is No Excuse p.67
The Loud Cry of Silent Wounds p.69
Now Love p.73
Did You p.75
Beauty Is a Reflection of I Am p.77
Out of The Closet I Came p.81
Who's Your Baby's Daddy p.83
Healed-Anointed- Revived p.85
Back Into The Fire p.87
True Love Waits p.89
Heartaches p.91
Overcomer p.93
The Mask Is Off p.95
The Battle Is Over p.97
A Letter to My Beautiful Reflections p.99

Acknowledgements

To my six beloved children: Darin Utley, Lamar C. Utley, DeAtra Taylor, E. Taron Utley, Tyra Browning and Antonio Utley we made it. I love you and I thank you so much for being honest but, most of all, for your forgiveness.

To my siblings: Cynthia Utley, William Utley, and Pastor Kerwin Utley- what can I say, tough love is what you gave, and because of that, I am now a better, much better person. I love you.

To Frank Bradford. Frank you know what? You are the mostest! Claudia Melton, Sheila Jones, and Barbara Algee McGee; you've shown me, through the ups and downs, what real friendship is all about.

To the greatest parents: Claudia Utley and the late Elsa Utley. Thank you Mom for being the Proverbs 31 Woman, not just to me, but to all the lives you have passed and touched.

To the greatest of all poets: I thank you and love you for your words. Dr. Maya Angelou, you've been an awesome blessing.

A very special thank you to Bishop Joseph W. Walker III, Mt. Zion Baptist Church– Nashville, for getting me ticked because you were "all in my business". It was exactly what I needed.

Foreword

"For I know my transgressions, and my sin is always before me"
- PSALM 51:3 -

A lot of things have been said about P. Utley Bradford over the years. Things that none of us would want to have said about us; no parent would want to have said about their daughter, or child have said about their mother.

There is an old saying: *"your reputation precedes you"*. This book is about Pam's reputation- How she got it; how she embraced it; how it almost took her life; how it affected the lives around her; and how Jesus saved her from it.

That may sound like a simple explanation of what you are about to read, but this is hardly simple reading. These poems were written throughout Pam's life as she was experiencing hurt, pain, abuse, and the chastening of God. The emotions of each poem are raw and true to what she felt at the time.

In the spirit of David, whom scripture says was a man after God's own heart P. Utley Bradford has produced the Psalms of her life in a way that could only be anointed by God. - *The Editor* -

"She that hath ears to hear, let her hear."

Introduction

In the Bible, the Apostle Paul asks what would seem to be a very simple question: *"Who shall separate us from the love of Christ?"* (Romans 8: 35) But when you are young and know nothing more about life than the love and care of a mother and father, you really don't understand why the old folk sing so much about leaning on Jesus and faith in God. I found out those reasons earlier in life than I expected.

I didn't know how precious I was to God. I didn't realize what my decisions meant to my family. I didn't understand the long term ramifications of my choices and actions. But that is part of being young and why it is all so very important for parents to not just sing the praises of Jesus, but to prepare their children for the realities of life.

As much as I have spent a lifetime wrestling with my youth, I was recently pinned down by the truth that, in a lot of ways, I wasn't really prepared for the very things I blamed myself for. I needed to forgive myself for being naive and young, forgive those who violated my innocence, and those who did not know to prepare me for my own protection. This was a big change from me taking the blame alone for so many years.

The burden of guilt, shame, and blame can blind you to the victory in Jesus. It can lead you to a life of sorrow where you never fully realize that the moment you understood your place with Him, that you were free from the chains that bind. Yet so many of us who follow Christ, do so dragging clinking chains. These chains are bound to things that separate us from fully realizing the love of God.

Paul also wrote *"For now we see through a glass, darkly; but then face to face: now I know in part; but then shall I know even as also I am known."* (1 Corinthians 13:12) This passage can be looked at in a lot of different ways. But if you can imagine the dark glass as a distant mirror that you are trying to reach; and guilt as the chains that keep you from reaching it, then at a distance, all you can see is the motion in the mirror. You have to get closer to recognize yourself. When you are able to come face to face with who you are, you are able to better know who you belong to.

This book is my walk toward the mirror. So many things in life can separate you from the love of Christ if you let it. Sickness, relationships, jobs, bills, family, children. Each poem is a broken link from the chains that bound me and separated me from Christ. *"For now I know even as I am also known"* (1 Corinthians 13:12) that *"in all things we are more than conquerors through him who loved us."* (Romans 8:37)

In my mirror now stands the generations of my choices. No longer a reflection of my sins, but of we who are *"fearfully and wonderfully made"* (Psalm 139:14) in the image of our heavenly father. In my mirror are 6 grown children ages 21 to 45, four of which are men. The grandmudder (as they lovingly call me) of 23 and the great grand of 7 boys and 1 granddaughter. I am also blessed to be married for 5 years to a man I have known since kindergarten.

I have come face to face with my darkened glass to find a reflection of love there waiting for me: from God, from my children, from my family, and for myself. It is my sincerest prayer that by bringing my mirror closer to you, that you will see yourself just as loved by God and seek His face in your own now darkened glass. **B**

14 | Can You See Yourself

PoeSermontry

1| MY MINISTRY

Oh Lord
Let me stay humble
in all you have me to do
As I send the 3 praises up
I know in my spirit
that pleases you
I'm not concerned
about fortune
I'm not concerned
about fame
For I'm already
rich and famous
I'm an heir
who carries your name
I pray in my Ministry
I can reach just one soul
For it's never me
that's speaking
But the spirit
who's taken control
My dream was to be
a Mahalia Jackson
Having a Ministry in song
But you pulled me
to the side and said

16 | Can You See Yourself

My child
you have it all wrong
A poetry ministry
is my will for you
So tell your testimonies
in poems
Help someone else
to make it through
I know some poems
will be hard my child
I know your pain
In knowing someone
may be helped
may eliminate
some of your shame

II| A DOVELY CONVERSATION

I've been afraid
to go out my front door
for several weeks
As I peek out today,
I hear this bird speak
"Let me introduce myself,
I'm the Dove from above,
and you are?"
You know I've been traveling
for over 2000 years
and I've only come this far
Look closely,
don't you recognize?
I ascended
on the shoulder of Jesus,
whom John baptized
I was there before,
when God sprinkled the night,
blanketed the earth,
and painted the sky blue
You're not the only one
that came over on the boat
I was on the Ark,
led in two by two
I'm here

18 | Can You See Yourself

to do you no harm,
for I come in peace
Remember
I was there
when the Holy Spirit
was released
I've been used
as a symbol of peace
Instead you want to hate
You need to turn to God,
fast and in a hurry
before it's too late
Even though his beak
never moved,
I heard every word
If a donkey can speak,
and rocks cry out,
then why can't I hear
from a bird?

III| AN HEIR

You ask Me
who I am?
I'm Spirit
Covered in
Beautiful black skin
I'm Nature
Sometimes changing
More often than I want
I'm Generations
Claudia yesterday
Pam today
Tyra tomorrow
I'm Patience
Sometimes having too much,
Other times not enough.
You ask me
Who I am?
I'm Life
Reproducing
Five lovely spirits
On loan from God.
I'm Flesh
Fighting with myself
To do what I know is right.
I'm Joy

20 | Can You See Yourself

So full,
Like bubbles
Overflowing a hot tub
I'm Peace
Lying out in God's grass
Gazing up at his twinkling stars
You ask me
Who I am?
I'm Pain
Hurting deep in my soul,
But thanking God for these days
I'm Light
Shining so bright,
You may not see my face
I'm Expressions
Just look at my face,
Have your questions been answered?
I'm Bones
Strong and sturdy,
Yet never dry
I'm Cotton
Soft as I want to be,
Yet still the Rock of Ages
I'm Water
Along with time
I'll destroy,
Yet you'll never thirst
I'm Thunder
Loud, but unseen.
I'm a Palm Tree
Swaying from side to side,

In My Mirror

Never breaking,
Never uprooted.
You ask me who I am?
I'm History
I'm an Underground Train rider
Yet front seat rider on the bus
You ask me
Who I am?
I'm a Pair of Moccasins
Wondering will you ever
Walk in my shoes
I'm Rape
Losing the fight,
But never becoming a victim
I'm Days
Realizing and accepting
That they are numbered.
You ask me
Who I am?
I'm Ears
Listening too often
To myself complain.
I'm Sight
Just looking to see
The Jesus in you
I'm Voice
Trying to say the right thing
I'm Feelings
Sometimes getting them hurt,
But gentle to the touch.
You ask me

Can You See Yourself

Who I am?
I'm an Heir of Salvation
My Father created
Heaven and Earth.
You ask me
Who I am?
I'm Time
Tick, Tocking to eternity
I'm Mortal
Headed to immortality
You ask me
Who I am?
I'm the Daughter
of All I Am's
You ask me
Who I am?
I Am
HIS

IV | UNDER RECONSTRUCTION

My appetite did dwindle;
I had no desire to eat
Don't worry about
Your earthly body;
My word is full of meat
My eyes began to get out of focus,
I could hardly see
Be still my child,
I'll clear your eyes,
See your focus is on me
My head is hurting often,
No peace this head could find
A voice cried out,
Keep holding on
I'm regulating your mind.
My hands looked pale,
And I could tell
My blood was very thin;
Don't matter about your blood,
I shed mine for you back then
My ears began to tingle
Oh Lord,
What can this tingling be?
I'm only trying
To get your attention,

24 | Can You See Yourself

That tingling you feel is me
At work I got light headed,
Nearly passed out;
I'm draining you,
And filling my spirit
A spirit that carries no doubt.
In a no-win relationship,
Temporary though it may be;
Just drop him Pam,
And pick me up
I'm with you
Through eternity
My clothes began
To hang off of me,
Hardly anything to wear;
I have your robe,
Wings and crown,
To place on your glorious hair
I felt as though I was dying,
As I watched
The going down of the sun;
My child
I was reconstructing you,
Now let's walk
Together as one

𝒱| THE DEVIL GOES TO CHURCH

Never told my parents
What happened
That dark and ugly day
How all my jewels were fondled,
I couldn't grant myself to say
As mom stood on the porch,
He brought me home past dark
Making up this crazy excuse,
Frozen, my life did park
I never told my story,
Didn't want to hurt anyone
All of a sudden,
My life took a wrong turn,
Because of what he'd done
Knowing what he did was wrong,
But somehow I felt
this strange urge
Later giving myself away,
My life took a downward surge
It was like an addiction,
Something my body had to feel
Didn't do no drugs,
Didn't drink,
But this addiction was so real.
Mr. Church man stole my jewels,

26 | Can You See Yourself

This definitely was not my choice.
Hindsight said I should have told,
My folks and given it a voice.
I should've, could've, would've,
My God, what have I done?
Afraid my dad would kill him,
My excuses stayed on the run.
So my addiction became man,
And his worldly touch
At the well, Jesus told me
All about myself
I love Him so very much.
In reaching in my mess,
He turned me inside out.
He pruned me, and cleaned me
His name brings about a shout
So five men later, and their love
I could never measure.
The Lord said "I am the giver of new life
And heavenly treasures"
Now he's the main man in my life,
For him I'll praise, sing, and dance
Who would not serve this amazing God,
The God of another chance
I now must tell my story,
For the hurting babies I will search
Everyone that worships
May not be Godly,
For even The Devil
Goes to Church

VI | STOLEN TREASURES

Hey Mister
Yes you, right there
Don't even turn away your head
You've raped my mind
You molested my heart
You sir
Killing my very stead
But, somehow, I felt free
I had choices in life
You took them all away
It's so hard with this lifestyle
But I'm coming clean today
Have you any idea
What all you put me through?
Folk calling me out of my name
Fag, Sweetie, and Homo too
Now folk will know your name
And all the boys and girls,
Your ugliness did touch.
You would not have gotten away
With this behavior
For you've stolen so very much
I've been spit at, hit on
Ridiculed and bullied too
Do you see all the hardship you've caused?

28 | Can You See Yourself

Dark days are headed for you
I need people to know
For I'm sure,
I'm not the only one
I pray this never happens,
To your daughter and or son
Your face is what I see
As I close my eyes to sleep
Praying there's not
Another in the daycare.
That you're trying to keep
God is working on me.
I'm trying to forgive
I've tried to take my life twice
Some days are much harder to live
There is so much more to me
Than what you've taken away
Lord help me, let go and forgive
For I'm becoming a man today
I lean not into my own understanding
He said he'd never leave me alone
Lord, only you can help me
Make this change.
Before my journey home

VII | BROKEN IN ALL THE RIGHT PLACES

God's tears
fell from the Heavens
upon my shattered face
My child
your small broken pieces
scatter this empty place
Your heart
will become naked,
for all the world to see
I'm molding the broken pieces
setting those demons free
You'll go through many changes,
still the darkness will unfold
For I am the Potter,
my chosen clay, I'll mold
I'll be the glue that mends,
your broken pieces together
No matter the day
or the season,
the time
or the weather
I will blow my Holy Spirit,
causing the glue to dry.
With the heat

Can You See Yourself

there will be some purging;
I'll heed your every cry
Broken pieces are all together
Many won't like what they see
If they have any complaints,
direct them straight to me
I am the Potter,
and thou art the clay
I'll mold and make you,
in my own way
With the Spirit
blown in you,
every piece will stay in place
Now on the mountain top,
broken pieces,
not a trace
Once the Lord mends
your broken pieces,
you'll never be the same
I was broken
In all the right places
Now, I'm mended
in Jesus' name
Unlike Humpty Dumpty,
I'm all back
together again
Thank you Potter and Spirit
for my broken pieces,
you did mend

VIII | LOVE TOOK A RIDE

We were all dressed up,
My sister Cynthia,
And her best friend.
Not knowing
I'd take a wrong turn
Down a dark street,
I would end
If you love me,
You won't fight me,
For you know,
I love you too
All I could think about,
Was hurry up,
And get through.
I felt so different inside,
I'm sure
It showed on my face
Not knowing the hurt
I would cause,
I felt so out of place
I washed, I washed,
I scrubbed, I scrubbed;
Nothing seemed to do
Lord, I can't
Talk to anyone about this.

Can You See Yourself

Please, can I talk to you?
Lord, I went against all I was taught,
I saw my world coming to an end.
Not realizing
Where this ride took me,
Nor realizing what lay within
Morning sickness was so bad,
I hardly hid mine
Knowing soon my figure would change,
Pam, you're running out of time
Mom and Dad found out.
Were you waiting
For your day of delivery?
I saw their hurt,
I felt their pain.
But also, I felt free.
So, the day came
We had to leave.
See My Daddy was shooting pool.
All I could ask,
What was on your mind,
you were such a fool.
Sixteen and in delivery,
Four hours seemed like a long long while.
Suddenly, it was all over,
They brought forth my first boy child
He was so perfect.
Perfect in every way.
A baby having a baby?
This baby,
Became a mother that day

In My Mirror

Ecclesiastes tells us,
There is a time and place for everything.
Giving birth
Will have its time,
But, not at age sixteen
You ask me,
What happened to his Dad?
Don't you even bother.
He denied my son,
"I'm not the one,"
"I am not your son's father"
Needless to say,
There came a day
My little son,
Now, a proud man
Here comes his dad,
Chest all stuck out,
Like he had a hand.
So remember girls,
Be at your best,
Try hard and refrain.
When love comes
to take you for a ride,
Cry out No!!!
In Jesus Name

I got over my anger with my son's father and he began to visit and take him for the summer. I had to forgive him. He was my son's Father. They ended up having a very beautiful relationship. Ladies, let's not bad mouth our children's fathers. After all, we did choose them. Remember God is also forgiving you on a daily basis.

IX | THE "3" I THOUGHT I KNEW

I don't have all the pieces
Some just don't fit
It was the night of our party
By the 3 I did get hit
I tried so hard to erase
What happened back in "68
For these guys
I thought were my friends
Neither of them my date
Never uttered a word about this
About what happened to me
It's hard enough being hit by one
See I was hit by 3
I was a youngster with one son
Another to be born someday
How could someone
Treat you like that
How can they treat you that way
I couldn't say anything
About the hit
I held it all inside
Maybe one day I can forgive
But the hurt is still alive
So guys take a listen
Take heed to what I say

36 | Can You See Yourself

Two of you have girls of your own
Pray they don't get hit that way
You'll never know how you've changed
My life some 28 years ago
Be still you 3 stop and listen
I'd love to tell you so
I know somehow I'll find pleasure
In knowing you'll pay for what you did
Making me feel ashamed
Guilty and dirty
So I ran and hid
I kept it all inside me
Like I was the one to blame
Too afraid to tell my parents
See I was so ashamed
Not only did you take
A precious part of me
Do you understand the void you left
Do you understand you 3
So when you stop and talk to me
Like nothing ever took place
Can you see the pain
I'm asking you why
More questions on my face
Now there is nothing I can't do
I'm reaching for the sky
But when I lay down
To take my last breathe
I'll still be asking
Why

✗| LIVING PHAT

I looked for love
In all the wrong places
Giving up my treasures
In very dark spaces
Necking, petting
And French kissing
In these, I took part
Not only did I hurt my Parents;
But, I broke the Lord's heart
Believing in my heart
That no one would know
Yet inside my immature body
A life began to grow
For six long scary months
I hid this inside
Afraid to tell my Parents
So, I continued to lie
Oh what an ugly place
For anyone to be
My Mom and Dad
Only wanting
The very best for me
Dirty diapers, no prom,
A crying baby
And formulas to fix

Can You See Yourself

Please,
Don't listen to Pookey them
For all he has is tricks
A trick to steal your treasures
To keep you bound inside
Let me tell you
Your sins from Christ
You can't hide
Abstain
Keep yourself pure
God will send Mr. or Miss Right
By abstaining, he'll take your lives
Marriage, and business
To higher heights.
A safe place
Is to stay
In Christ, and stay pure
Jehovah Jira
Your provider
With him you can endure
Endure, stand tall
Let Pookey know
What he's asking for
Is not divine.
For with God;
I'm Living Phat
Pursuing heaven
At all times

XI| DISAPPOINTED, NOT ANGRY

So you're upset with me
because of hard lessons
you had to learn
Being a page in my book
you've been read
now, you've been turned
Don't try and make me feel bad
like I'm some simple reject
I thought you were a real man
I've lost all respect
Had many good times
in this chapter;
now on to chapter two
I hope the writing on the wall
is clear enough for you
There have been others
in my life
not bragging
just plain facts
Your train has left the station,
Disappearing down the tracks
So this book is finished
another soon to start
You brought upon yourself
rainy days
but forgot to build your Ark

40 | Can You See Yourself

XII | HER APPLE BUT YOUR CHOICE

You people
Make me sick
You've tasted
The forbidden fruit
You did
What you wanted to do
Now it's not so cute
You walk around all day
With this funky attitude
Treating everyone
Mean, nasty
And very rude
You have control
Over your needs
And what you want to do
Now you point the finger,
Everyone's wrong but you
You were man enough
To do what you did
Now your mouths stuck out
You're acting like a kid
Maybe you've learned
A valuable lesson,
When some other you'll meet

Can You See Yourself

Think about your status
Let your desires
Take a back seat
You knew you were married
I just can't pass her by
Your flesh says go for it
My spirit cries why
I know I wasn't the first,
Sure won't be the last
I hear you're seeing Ms. Lady
Are you?
A question
I needed to ask
I have no malice against you,
For lust is there no longer
Going thru what
I put myself thru,
This Sista
Is much
Stronger

XIII | NOT SO PRETTY

Pretty woman, is nothing new
I've been there
A time or two
Sure, not bragging or anything
I got clothes, dinner
And a diamond ring
Paid for Ms. Lady
To do my hair
Before I turned around
I'm sitting in her chair
Never had to want for much
Never having him to touch.
As long as I was showered with gifts
That's all fine
Never wanting to give up
Anything of mine
See pretty is, as pretty does
Pretty, I no longer was
I knew I had to pay the piper
It's payday
Never thought pretty woman
Would go out that way
See, never bite off
More than you can chew
Cause the Holy Spirit
Will get the best of pretty you

44 | Can You See Yourself

XIV | I NEARLY TALKED MYSELF TO DEATH

I nearly
talked myself to death
by speaking down to my life
I can't do this or that
bad times
much grief
and strife
Always sitting on
my blessed assurance
Crying about what's not
Sista girl
don't even go to Church
but look at all she's got
People said
I won't amount to much
Waddling in the dirt
she'll always be
I got to believing
everything they said
I had no confidence in me
Bishop said
life and death is in the tongue
You need only
wash your mouth out

46 | Can You See Yourself

He said
your destiny is established
What on earth
are you crying about
Bishop said
you can live life
or life can live you
So speak those things
that be not
as though they were
That's what you need to do
Right then
I searched the scriptures
I'm a conqueror
fearfully and wonderfully made
I'm the righteousness of God
His life for me he gave
Now a great appetite
for my Jesus
he delivered me from the waves
of the stormy sea
Oh taste and see
that God is good
His angels are encamped around me
Oh magnify the Lord with me
and forever exalt his name
For he is no respecter of person
For you
He will do
The same

𝑋𝑉 | ALL UP IN MY BUSINESS JESUS SET ME UP

I was
that Woman
at the well
all deep in my mess
a sad but true story
one I must daily confess
another Man
sitting at the well
waiting for my body and me
please give me a drink of water
a different approach, I see
I'm a Samaritan woman
and you are a Jew
He offered a free gift
He's after me
I just knew
those that drink of my water
shall never thirst again
As I looked into His eyes
I saw a different kind of Man
He said, "Go and get your husband
and come right back"
a husband of my own
well, that's something that I lacked

Can You See Yourself

what about Robert,
Earl, Kirk, Steve, and FB?
it seemed as if He looked
straight through me
all in my kool-aid
all up in my mess
but no husband of my own
the truth I did confess
they gave me beautiful children
and they said they loved me too
I'll be with you thru all eternity
that's something
none of them could do
Now I looked backed that day
in a conversation with De,
Bold Betty
is what I call her
for that Sista's bold as she can be
Mom
God wakes you every morning
with health, strength
and a little change
He does all He can for you
yet fornication, adultery, and lust
still remain
He gave you life itself
but you sigh
and remain in your sin
my question is
what will it take
for He alone

knows your end
It ended that day
He delivered me from the fall
and all that mess
for He's tailoring my robe
and burning my harlot's dress
all that you went through
my child
was not just for you
go in and bring others out
that's what I want you to do
now, I'm here to tell you
this Sista drinks
from a different cup
for He was all in my business
Thank God
Jesus set me up

Deliverance is sweet

50 | **Can You See Yourself**

XVI | THE GARDENER

In slavery days,
the father was snatched away
Fast forward to today;
the father has no desire to stay
He believes he is a gardener
planting his seed to go
Off to the next garden,
planting row,
after row, after row
Can't just blame the man,
for she should protect her own
Wrote a song about it,
want to hear it,
"Papa was a rolling stone"
There is nothing funny
about a child not knowing his father
Explain mom,
why I act this way?
but she doesn't even bother.
My heart consist of 4 chambers,
cause of you, one is unable to work
All I hear my mom ever say,
"he was such a jerk"
It takes two to tangle,
so moms don't talk bad about him

Can You See Yourself

For in the game of lust,
no one ever wins
Women, stop putting
your baby on Jim,
when you know
he's really Fred's
Your problem is,
you thought no one knew
you were slipping
in and out of beds
Let's take this donor thing,
and kick it up a level
Sleeping around
has never been cool,
especially with the Devil

Who plants in your garden?

XVII | THIS IS MY STORY NOT A PRETTY SONG

I was abused
at 13 years old
A very upsetting situation,
One my parents- I never told.
Then at 15, RC decided
we should become one
March 16th, I delivered
a healthy and beautiful son
Now, I was branded as a fast
and very ugly little girl
Feeling I was the only one,
who had made a mistake
in this world.
At 17, raped by three
I thought were my friends
It was my very first party,
a sad way for it to end
Now being told
I'd never amount to much,
I wasn't worth the time of day
Jesus said,
"It was I who made you,
and washed your sins away"
So my addiction

54 | Can You See Yourself

turned out to be
Man,
thinking they were men
Misused, beaten up, raped,
Walked on time
and time again
I remember one day
a 357 was placed at my head
Will I be covered in my own blood?
Will I be pronounced dead?
When will this all end?
For in my heart and soul
I feel much disgrace
Five sets of sad eyes,
tears of fear,
run down my baby's face.
Don't for one minute ever think
your actions
won't affect your kids life
I wanted my addiction to stop
so badly,
wanting to be
a real man's wife
Let's cut to the chase,
skip down to 2001,
Dec. 27 to be exact
"I'm delivering you
from your addiction,
no good thing
from me you'll lack."
The past was very ugly,

my life running
rapidly out of control.
"No one can love you like I do,
for I am
the lover of your soul"
Now working at Springhill Suites,
ironic as it maybe,
for my eyes are now opened
from my addiction
I am free
Is this a test, for I'll never resort
back to my old way
"Well done with me
in eternity",
I will hear my Savior say

56 | Can You See Yourself

XVIII | NO LONGER NASTY

Do you lay back
and let all the women in your life
take care of you in everyway?
Did you see your Mom
take care of her man
back in the day?
Do you run out
looking for a hit in the alley,
the streets, and houses every where?
Now your family's
giving tough-love
you cry to everyone
thinking no one cares
Your Nasty is?
Is your nose up in the air
as you step on folk
as you think
you're reaching the top?
Do you realize the same folk
you stepped on you'll see
as you begin to drop?
Are you laying
with Sally's husband,
she's your so called
Sista and best friend?

58 | Can You See Yourself

Are you fornicating and lusting
with men, after men, after men?
Your Nasty is?
Are you talking about Miss Lady
as the Lord blesses her with a house
and debt free car?
Instead of rejoicing with her
and praising God,
you are jealous when
your blessings weren't that far.
Instead of getting you a job,
let's just rob the Pizza Man
and take all he's got
Knowing your stupid actions
only get you
3 meals and a cot
Your Nasty is?
Now stop it,
Nasty Women,
Stop it
Nasty Man
Drop to your knees,
lay on your face,
cry to Jesus
for His Almighty hand.
See I was
that Nasty Girl
fornicating, lying and cheating,
a woman with no plan
Jesus delivered and placed
his anointing on me

He's my lover and only
Faithful Man.
Now stand on my promises,
pray my scriptures back to me
I'm a God that cannot lie,
You are my Queen
with an upward destiny
Destined to take my word
to the highway and byways
across this Nasty World.
By me, you are blessed
and highly favored
All things are possible,
No longer
a nasty girl

60 | **Can You See Yourself**

XIX | THE OLD FASHIONED WAY

To plant a seed
And make a baby
It's not hard to do
In raising a child
And loving on him
Much is required of two
God's plan for us
Is to marry
Spend quality time
With our spouse
Before we bring
The sound of pitter patter
All through the house
The plan started in Genesis
Started with Adam and Eve
For Adam
To find his mate
To her alone he'd cleave
God is a God
Of His word
Nothing He said
Has changed
He marries him
She marries her
His word

Can You See Yourself

Was not rearranged
God said be of one wife
Not two, three or more
You decided
To do it your way
Opening wide Hell's door
Try the old fashion way
And find yourself
A good wife
Love on her,
Have some babies
And live
a Godly life

XX | TURN THE WORLD OFF

Lord
you said
your sheep
will hear
and heed
it's Master's voice.
And rightly so
My child,
for everything in life
is about choice
Lord
can you
maybe
speak louder?
Your voice
I cannot hear
Turn off the T.V.
settle the kids
for I am speaking
loud
and clear.
Lord
I need help!
You said
you were my Father

64 | Can You See Yourself

and I your little girl
I am a God
that cannot lie
you need only
turn down
the world.
I am
Jehovah Shamah
in your heart and soul
I can be found
If you can't hear Me
loud and clear,
you need only
turn
the world's volume
down

XXI| NOT YOURS

I knew all the scriptures
and I sang all the songs
but for three long days and nights
something went
terribly wrong
I stayed in my room
crying out for my Jesus
crying for my Lord
He rocked me
My child My way is right
but often seems hard
I felt as though
I'd been drinking
from a bitter cup
wanting to throw
in the towel
wanting to die
wanting to give up
I even contemplated
taking my own life
what was I living for
Holy Spirit said
how can you
take something
that is

Can You See Yourself

Not Yours
Lord God please
forgive me
for entertaining the thought
for thinking that way
according to Your Word
Your mercy's are new
each and everyday
You see Saints
I'm on a faith walk
finding my purpose
doing my Master's will
Satan's going to and fro
my soul he wants
so badly to steal
I was gonna
give up everything
for around the corner
I could not see
I woke up
got up
and I'm walking
in My Victory

XXII | THERE IS NO EXCUSE

December 29th
I felt your pain
You were really sad
"Mom, did I have to go away?"
"Was I really that bad?"
You and Dad got together
And conceived me
Dad said he felt closed in
He wanted to be free
So that left you and me
Mom, we weren't alone
"So why did you did this?"
When I was your very own
You just found out about me
Four weeks ago.
I thought you'd be happy together
In love we'd grow
"Why didn't you give me a chance
To be all I could be?"
I know we could have been happy
Just you and me.
There is no good reason
No Excuse
For what you did
You never gave me a chance

68 | Can You See Yourself

To be that wonderful kid
Ms. Mary up the street,
tried for years to become a Mother
So many can't conceive,
For one reason or another.
You could've given me
up for adoption
then started your life again.
But you chose to snuff mine out
before my life would begin,
Today I'd be grown,
And, of course, a great asset
You only thought of yourself
and getting your own needs met
There Is No Excuse

XXIII | THE LOUD CRY OF SILENT WOUNDS

Thirty odd years later
the silent wounds speak:
Mom you missed my games
I broke records
while you broke my heart
I caught passes
while you kept passing me by
I made touch downs
while you never built me up
Mom, where were you?
My kisses my hugs
Mom, who'd you give them to?
I craved a simple, "I love you"
Yet bottles of pain
are locked in the chambers
of my heart, heading toward
permanent residence
Was I not worthy
of your love and time?
Could you not hear the pain?
For it screamed loudly and daily
out of my every pore
Could you not smell
the fragrance of loneliness?

Can You See Yourself

Or did the English Leather
take control of your nostrils
Mom, where were you?
Could you not see
your baby needed you?
No! all you could see was
the imitation of a man
who was taking my time
There are things in my life
that will forever be painful and silent
Never having a childhood;
cause you traded in my early years
for your late nights
Mom, being honest
I felt only the opposite of love for you
I would have given up
games, toys, bikes, and Skateland
Just to be loved and hugged
Today Mom, the silent wounds speak
God is giving us the time
to unlock the silence
and take off the band aids
so our wounds can heal
Heal only by the soft, sweet breeze
of the Holy Spirit
The child and the mother;
were both wounded, wounding others
not only from heart to heart
but from person to person
from city to city
from my door steps to yours

You see the silence of the wounded
was so loud it echoed up
Silently knocking on the door of glory
and God heard
the loud cry
of the silent wound

72 | **Can You See Yourself**

XXIV | NOW LOVE

I couldn't give
what I never accepted
for myself
I couldn't give out
what wasn't within
And because of
my self-flicked wounds
I wounded you
Forgiveness?
Do you remember the time….
Or maybe it was…..
Can you pinpoint the day……
Shelter – food – clothes – toys
and lights sometimes were out
Football games
Football games
Talent shows
Football games
Track and field
Can you tell me who?
Why was there always
an empty seat?
I understand
why dad wasn't there
Where were you?

74 | Can You See Yourself

I'll tell you where you were
Locked
in the lust chamber
of your own selfishness
I was NFL
The next Patti LaBelle
My name rang loud
in the halls
because of records broken
The only record
you ever cared for
was "Sexual Healing"
and "Just Let Me Love You Tonight"
It was always night for you
but Joy
has come this morning
all wrapped in forgiveness
Mom,
I forgive you
forgive yourself
Now
Love

XXV | DID YOU

Ever wonder why?
Ever wonder who?
Who was making me
feel uncomfortable
As a little girl?
As a little boy?
While you were giving love
In all the wrong places
To all the wrong faces
Why was I
attracted to older women?
Why was I
attracted to older men?
Why did I
stay down their house?
Why did I
ride my bike
18 miles in the cold rain?
Why did we
go into the military?
Why did I lean more?
To my dad's family?
Did You ever wonder?

Did you?

76 | **Can You See Yourself**

XXVI | BEAUTY IS A REFLECTION OF I AM

You're asking Me
for an anointed,
wealthy and fine man
Your prayers
are being answered,
now let's see
where you stand
Your feet have racked up
many miles,
traveling in and out
of the wrong place
Now shod with my preparation,
you walk in my favor,
In my amazing grace
Your hands
traveled even further
doing ugly things
only you and I know
Beautiful hands,
anointed hands
now touch My people
wherever they go.
This door,
shows how you

Can You See Yourself

treated my temple,
watch your steps
ugliness is piled
all over the floor.
Lord, to look inside myself
is making me ill,
I just can't walk
thru another door.
Forgive me, Lord
for all the wrong I've done,
ugly Pam is all I see
I've renewed your mind,
cleaned up your heart,
your beauty now lies in me
My child,
I'm not a genie,
I don't grant wishes,
for you were always in my will.
Continue looking up
and don't go back
for joy, in my heart you've filled.
I said I'd give you
the desires of your heart.
My child,
this I'll surely do
Prepare yourself
your prayers have been answered,
your king is headed for you
Lord, this is like the Christmas story;
Christmas future, Christmas present
and Christmas past

Child, this is My Son's story
and what you do for him
is gonna last.
Old things have past away
behold all things have become new
Your ministry, husband, and mansion
are a few blessings
I'm pouring out on you
Father God,
thanks for showing
my past ugliness that lay inside.
Now you've been
cleaned up by the master,
only beauty can reside
When complimented,
stay humble
and know I am
that inside light
I'll pray and praise you,
meditate on your word
both day and night
Oh Lord, I will open my lips
and my mouth
shall shew forth thy praise.
My tongue shall sing aloud
thy righteousness
the rest of my blessed days
Look back, but press toward the mark
speaking those things
that be not as though they were.

80 | **Can You See Yourself**

XXVII | OUT OF THE CLOSET I CAME

I turned the knob
and from the closet
I came out
For in hell I lifted my eyes,
I've something to shout about
Had no problem with Sunday,
out of the closet I would come
Monday thru Saturday
back in, I'd quickly run
Now, I call daily on a higher power,
Jesus is his name
I am not ashamed of the Gospel,
no shame in my game
Think About This:
What if Sunday was the only day
you'd see Christ in me?
Then Monday thru Saturday
you see me,
fraternizing with the enemy
What if Christ
was in the closet Friday,
when the magnum
was pointed at my head?
I'd just be another statistic,

82 | Can You See Yourself

pushing up daisies instead
What if Christ
was in the closet Monday
and my heart surgery was due?
Who'd be with the Dr.'s ?
Who'd be with my family?
who would bring me thru
I heard Him say,
"I'm Jehovah Jira
your provider,
in a closet I'd never be"
I Am
healed all thy diseases,
I Am
forgave all you iniquities
My mercy is new every morning
from everlasting to everlasting
I am an on time God,
you have not b'cause
you're not asking
I am a peculiar people,
a royal priesthood,
praising him everyday
I am out of the closet
and out I'm going to stay
Blessed the Lord, Oh my soul
and all that is within me,
bless his holy name
For such a time as this
Out of the closet I came

XXVIII | WHO'S YOUR BABY'S DADDY

My life
was
a labor of pain
pushing
panting
contracting
agonizing
and calling out
to God
in despair
he heard my cry
Pam time to push
my water broke
living water
then the blood
His blood
covering our babies
I was delivered from
I was delivered to
from sexual sins
To my purpose
I gave birth to triplets
one for the Father
one for the Son

Can You See Yourself

one for the Holy Spirit
Time to nurse
nursing intercessory prayer
nursing PoeSermontry
nursing his prophetic word
now I spend my days
loving on my 3 precious babies
showing them off to everyone I meet
Why you ask
cause I am a proud momma
the lover of my soul
impregnated me
before I was even a thought
my questions for you are
Are you pregnant?
Will your labor be induced?

Who's your Baby's Daddy?

XXIX | HEALED - ANOINTED REVIVED

I remembered Monday night,
I left earth for a while.
"I've healed and anointed you
so go back
go back my blessed child"
I've increased your measure of faith;
much more is required of you,
"Now keep your feet
shod with my Gospel,
and I will carry you through"
I'm walking,
leaping and praising God
Sounds like a very simple thing
For if you keep
His word ever present
what comfort the Spirit will bring
I can't explain what happened
a miracle- a mystery to me
My God does work in mysterious ways,
for He has set this captive free
He's cleaned up
this old messy house,
leaving this big open space
I'll fill it up

Can You See Yourself

with love, joy and peace,
my fruits are now in place
You see my world
did burn within
as He spoke to me,
one on one.
"Remember
what's required of you,
more blessings
are yet to come"
So study to show myself approved,
Lord, let me never be ashamed
Whatever I do
in the days to come,
I'll do it in Jesus name
"I've told you to go and minister
all across this sin filled land,
get ready, get started, get loose,
time to take a soldier's stand"
I trust in you and lean not,
not unto my own,
so I'll have to make a move,
for this house is not my home
If you see me acting strange,
Try counting the tear drops that fall
I'm seeing my Savior on Calvary,
my Jesus did pay it all.
I'll forever press toward the mark
He alone my spirit heed
For Lord, you are my Shepherd,
you're all I'll ever need

𝒳𝒳𝒳 | BACK INTO THE FIRE

I saw her
in the fire,
I heard her
scream, her shout
God chose me
as his caring servant
to go bring my sista out
I saw her
body burning
addictions and lust
consumed her air
I knew God
and I could help her,
for I'd already
been there
As we embraced and cried,
the Lord led us to the light
We three knelt and prayed,
see with God all things
are made right
As we ministered
to her physical body,
she got her strength back
Then, God fed her
His word saying,

Can You See Yourself

"No good thing from Me you'll lack"
I shared my testimony
of all the hell
I put myself through
If God can save
a wretch like me,
it's no secret
what He can do
There was an abortion,
the magnum,
the knife,
truck cables
and raped
by 3 so-called friends
Yes, I made it
through the fire,
now I celebrate
my miraculous end
I chose to go back
into the fire,
to help bring my Sistas out.
From their addictions,
fornication, adultery and lust
to show what real love's about.
I deliberately go back
into the intense heat,
the fire, that's no joke
It's because of his grace and mercy,
we came out
with no smell of smoke

𝒳𝒳𝒳𝐼 | TRUE LOVE WAITS

For God so love the world
that he gave;
Not for you to sneak around,
but for you to behave
So worship Him
in the beauty of his holiness.
Stay pure, stay holy so
you can be truly blessed.
Beloved, have his promise
and perfect holiness
in the fear of our Lord.
So when Pookey dem step to you,
you'll always be on guard.
Remember, whatsoever things are pure
and of a good report,
think on these things
continue to focus on God
He alone can fulfill
your wildest dreams;
Walk in your holiness and purity
asking the Lord to keep you night and day
For you know him as the author
and finisher of your faith.
His grace and mercy
is the only way

Can You See Yourself

The wisdom that is from above is pure,
peaceable, gentle and easy to be entreated
When peer pressure rears her ugly head,
stand firm let them know God
is all that's needed
Don't let Pookey dem,
speak sweet nothings
it's a trap
it's just bait.
Tell him, "I am the apple of God's eye"
His beloved, you see
True Love Waits
He'll try breaking you down,
for his only concern is personal pleasure
With boldness tell him,
"True Love Waits"
I'm holding on to my treasures
Be ye holy, for I am holy,
this is what the good book said
So lean not unto your own understanding,
by the Holy Spirit be lead
Always keep your focus on God,
for at the end of this life
he'll welcome you
thru his gate.
Abstain,
stay pure and holy
knowing with God

True Love Waits

XXXII | HEARTACHES

It's so hard to let go;
Even though you know
it's right to do
For with every
beat of your heart,
you ache, for they
are a part of you.
Lord, what to do
when your children
choose the wrong life to live?
More love,
more prayer
is what you should long to give
How do you
stop worrying?
Are they safe,
have they eaten?
Do they have a place to lay?
Lord, the pain seems so deep,
will it ever go away?
"What you are feeling
is so real,
it's the same way
I feel about you.
I want you

Can You See Yourself

to keep my commandments,
and some of them, you do"
"I want you to rest
and delight yourself in me.
You often turn
to look at others,
and the worldly things that be"
"I loved you 2000 years ago,
before your Mom
ever met your Dad
Love is to be a wonderful act
As I look upon the earth,
I'm made sad
Pam, you thought this writing
was for your children
Please look again"
"I, your Father,
love you so much
for my parenting
never ends
Now think on those things
that are lovely, honest
and those things
that are true.
Hand in hand
we'll travel this stage
of the journey,
remember,
I am carrying you"

XXXIII | OVERCOMER

Heard things like,
"you're a pretty chocolate girl"
"Chocolate is my flavor,
but does not darken my world"
"No man will want to marry
anyone dark like you"
Prejudice within the race,
just won't do
I would have been
one of the slaves
raped by the evil master
Wasn't that enough
to go through?
A living disaster
"Oh, what a beautiful face,
but she is so under weight"
Maybe she has a medical issue,
can you even relate?
Why does he talk like that?
"I can't understand
a word he said"
He was shot by a drive by,
a massive blow to his head
Before you open your mouth,
talk only what you know

Can You See Yourself

Remember, someone
is wondering about you,
and how you
so perfectly flow
We have such a bad habit
of judging folk,
before we even
know their name
Turn the mirror
on yourself,
aren't you the least
bit ashamed?
I know you think
you are all that
and a large bag of chips
You're just a day,
an hour away
from having your
own needs clipped
I have overcome
what you think,
or even what you
think you see
I'm rooted
and grounded
in Jesus,
being the best
me I can be

XXXIV | THE MASK IS OFF

masquerading
all over the place
looking
in the mirror
never recognizing
my own face
will the real me
step forward
shake off
all these fake days
as I step out of the mirror
even I am amazed
so many disguises
seems I've been confused
was it the rapes
or the beatings
different masks
I had to use
who was I
all those false yesterdays
were those my real actions
my real words
were those my
real ways
as I hide

Can You See Yourself

behind many yesteryears
in His name off comes
the last disguise
calling the name of Jesus
has lifted my spirit
and I've become wise
no more masquerading
what you see
is the real me
take me
or leave me,
don't matter
cause I've been set free
free from you telling me
who you think I am
I now know
what you were selling
just another scam
the Lord said
my beloved daughter
never cover
my awesome work of art
unmask your face,
cause your beauty lies
deep inside
your heart
the mask comes off
for the victory
is mine

XXXV | THE BATTLE IS OVER

I write
most of the time
out of my hurt,
wounds and pain
walking the streets
of nowhere
hearing voices
sounding insane
plan to take
a friends life
over a man
who was not mine
trying hard
to find my senses
as I journey
through life blind
looking back
on the day
I jumped from
the second floor
running
from my abuser
as I've done
so many times before
so many days

98 | Can You See Yourself

I had to run
never ready to die
I beseech thee my sistas'
stay away
so you won't be
asking why
I'm opening my heart
so you can see
the damage
wrong choices cause
don't let him tell you
you're not worth anything
it will put your life
on pause
I am now strong in the Lord
and in his might
Beloved step aside
I've got this
your battles
I'll surely fight
the hurt is gone
wounds are healed
I'm absent of the pain
I'm a new creature in Christ
I found victory
in His name
proud to be
a survivor of abuse
hear you asking me how
God was there in dangers unseen
my battle is over now

XXXVI | A Letter to My Beautiful Reflections

After reading what may seem like a lot of negative poetry, I just want you to know that God is no respecter of person. He really is a deliverer. I know now, that all I went through was not just for me, but for all the Beautiful Reflections in my mirror- you. God gave me the grace to go through all that, so I could come out and help rescue others.

I now thirst and hunger after righteousness, as I chase after my Savior. My first change was to learn to like and love myself. The Lord pruned all the bark off me. He showed me where I needed improving, then together we worked on it. A lot of my pruning had to do with my children.

My second son, and baby daughter showed me ugly Pam, me being absent when they really needed me. Not always telling them I loved them, and sometimes not showing it. All six of my children are my favorites, and each one brings a different dish to the table.

I love each and everyone with my whole heart. One thing I learned through my mistakes, they have become better parents and people. Lessons I learned through it all are, learn the love of God, then you can learn to love others. I couldn't give away what I didn't have.

In 1997, I started dating my now husband and best friend, whom I simply adore. My second change was prayer. Frank and I pray together daily. You say pray, and I want to drop to my knees and go for it. Upon rising in the morning, I go up to my prayer closet to pray and meditate, for at least an hour.

I belong to Christian Faith Fellowship Church in Milwaukee, WI, where Bishop Darrell L. and Pamela Hines are my covering. I belong to the Intercessory Prayer Ministry, the Nursing Home Ministry and on Tuesday evening, you can find me at Bible study.

Don't get me wrong, I still have a long way to go. I do know my latter days are greater than my former ones. I have stepped out of my mirror and now walk in the presence of my Lord and Savior.

My third change is worrying. God said, to bring your burdens to him and leave them there. It broke me up so bad, when my name was blowing on the wings of the morning.

Now I don't worry about what people may say about me, cause God said, "I am fearfully and wonderfully made", marvelous are his works. I am more than a conqueror, through Jesus Christ.

My heart specialist told me worry will only shorten your life. My valve replacement is 21 years old. To God be the glory.

God has always been apart of my life, now I know him to be the head of my life. He is so amazing.

Along with these changes, I have done my PoeSermontry in Champaign-Urbana, Decatur, Mattoon, and Rantoul Churches. In Nashville, TN, I worked with a group of ladies at Pastor Bryan Williams Church.

I was also blessed to do some motivational speaking at some schools here in Milwaukee. Look at God. PoeSermontry is my favorite thing to do. First, it is a word the Lord gave me. It means, there is a sermon in the poems I write.

A lot of wrong turns have been taken, but God- I thank God daily for lifting the burden of worry off me.

My fourth change, is being ever so thankful for all things. One of my favorite scriptures is, "Whatever state I am in, therewith, to be content". Hallelu-yer. I'm thankful for my parents teaching me about the love of God, training me in the way I should go, so when I am old I'll not depart from it.

Oh yes, I strayed, but it didn't take me long to get back on course. I am thankful to my children, for teaching me how to love and be a good mother.

Love the Utley 6. My siblings, for loving me in spite of my hard head. My honey, for being the man I needed to tame the beast in me, to love me at all times, and to communicate regardless.

Mainly, my Heavenly Father for giving me another chance, and another chance, and another

Can You See Yourself

chance. He is my Jehovah Jira, my Jehovah Shalome, my Jehovah Shammah, my Jehovah Gibbor, my ancient of days, my Lord of Lords, my strength when I'm weak, and he is my all and all.

My prayer for you, who are my Reflections, is, Lord, give them the strength to climb out of these negative situations. Give them the courage, to look in the mirror and see the Beauty that's within. Let them, with your help Lord, pull themselves up and get on to a life with you- life full of promises which they can stand strong on. God you are forever faithful.

You said, "We have not cause we ask not". Lord, we're asking for a changed life. We are going to lean not to our own understanding, but in all our ways acknowledge you. We need you Lord, every second, minute, hour, day, week, month, and year. Lord please, bring our real beauty to the forefront. Help us to move forward in you, in Jesus name we pray. Amen.

Time to get out of the mirror and into his presence. He'll walk with you, and talk with you. He will never leave you, nor forsake you. He will never tell your secrets. He will be everything you need. Most of all, he will be with you, always loving you unconditionally .

-P.Utley Bradford B